PORTRAITS OF POETS

FOR MY FATHER AND MOTHER

CHRISTOPHER BARKER

Portraits of Poets

EDITED BY SEBASTIAN BARKER

CARCANET

First published in Great Britain 1986 by
Carcanet Press Ltd
208-212 Corn Exchange Buildings
Manchester M4 3BQ

108 East 31st Street, New York
New York 10016

The publisher acknowledges the financial assistance
of the Arts Council of Great Britain

Barker, Christopher
Portraits of poets.
1. Photography — Portraits
2. Poets, British — 20th century — Portraits
1. Title 2. Barker, Sebastian
779'.2'0924 TR681.P/

ISBN 0-85635-651-4 Pbk
ISBN 0-85635-650-6

Designed by Richard Hollis and David King
Typesetting by Type Generation, London
Printed in England by Balding and Mansell,
Wisbech and London

The poets included in *Portraits of Poets* have been selected from those born in the first forty years of the century (1897-1939), writing and publishing in Ireland, Scotland, Wales and England. A definitive selection was impossible, partly because this seemed to me a job for the literary historians of the future; and partly because, in a book of photographs taken from life, there were those we would like to have included who were dead when the book was begun. Nevertheless, we focused attention on the nucleus of the poets, living and active during 1980-86 when *Portraits of Poets* was made. (The portrait of Patrick Kavanagh, taken shortly before his death in 1967, is one exception to this.)

The selection was drawn from several categories. There are those, for example, who attained considerable popular recognition during their lifetimes; those who have significance outside their own poetry through their influence on changing fashions; and those, of whom Paul Potts is perhaps the best example, who have known the full weight of neglect. There are the contributors to translation. And there are those, the majority, who make up the hard core of the poetic intelligence of the age.

We were not guided in this selection by any school or clique or theory of poetry retailing a scholastic fashion. *Portraits of Poets* is for the general public. It was not prepared for the specialist of the numerous facets of contemporary poetry (as numerous as there are poets to reflect them), but for the reader who takes an active interest in poetry yet feels at times the inhuman face of it in print. It was also made for the pupil and teacher, the student and lecturer. It was assembled to make the senior poets of our time more accessible, by showing them in straightforward, even biographical settings, with examples of their work and their autographs.

Christopher Barker took his bearings in his work from close reading of the poets' books, and considerations such as camera, film, lighting, and print development. Altogether, this involved six years' travel and research. Each poet required a different way of looking, a different technique.

Portraits of Poets presents the human face of an art sometimes obscured from general enjoyment and even intelligent appreciation by wilful mystification and academic tariff-barriers. We hope that the formally skilled and the informally talented, as well as those discovering poetry, might find here a useful point of departure. In any case, we wanted to pay tribute to our elder generations, placing on record this unique testimony to their spirit.

Sebastian Barker

10
SIR SACHEVERELL SITWELL
Born 1897, Yorkshire. Eton and Balliol College, Oxford.
Grenadier Guards, World War I. Writer on art and travel.
The People's Palace, 1918. Numerous collections. *Collected Poems*, 1936.
From 'The Turn of The World'

12
EDGELL RICKWORD
1898-1982. Born Essex. Colchester Grammar School and Pembroke College, Oxford.
Military Cross, World War I. Literary editor.
Behind the Eyes, 1921. *Collected Poems*, 1947.
Complaint After Psycho-Analysis

14
BASIL BUNTING
1900-1985. Born Northumberland.
Leighton Park School and London School of Economics.
Worked on *Transatlantic Review*; in Persia; on local Newcastle paper.
Briggflatts, 1966. *Collected Poems*, 1968.
From Part V of 'Briggflatts'

16
PATRICK KAVANAGH
1905-1967. Born Co. Monaghan, Eire. Writer.
Ploughman And Other Poems, 1936. Several collections. *Collected Poems*, 1964.
Wet Evening in April

18
GEOFFREY GRIGSON
1905-1985. Born Cornwall. St Edmund Hall, Oxford.
Founding editor *New Verse*, 1933-39; critic and anthologist.
Several Observations, 1939. Numerous collections. *Collected Poems*, 1982.
Thank You

20
SIR JOHN BETJEMAN
1906-1984. Born London. Marlborough and Magdalen College, Oxford.
Mount Zion, 1931. Numerous collections. *Collected Poems*, 1979. Poet Laureate
1972-1984.
The Last Laugh

22
SIR WILLIAM EMPSON
1906-1985. Born Yorkshire. Winchester and Magdalene College, Cambridge.
Taught at universities in Japan, China, America, and England.
Poems, 1935. *Collected Poems*, 1955.
From 'Autumn on Nan-Yueh'

24
JOHN LEHMANN
Born 1907, Buckinghamshire. Eton and Trinity College, Cambridge.
Editor *Penguin New Writing*, 1936-50, and *London Magazine*, 1954-1961.
A Garden Revisited, 1931. Several collections. *Collected Poems*, 1963.
Coming Into Your Room

26
KATHLEEN RAINE
Born 1908, London. County High School, Ilford, and Girton College, Cambridge.
Studies of William Blake and the Neoplatonic tradition.
Stone and Flower; Poems 1935-1943, 1943; numerous collections. *Collected Poems*,
1957.
Afternoon Sunlight Plays

28
SIR STEPHEN SPENDER
Born 1909, London. University College School and University College, Oxford.
Co-editor *Horizon*, 1939-41, *Encounter*, 1953-67. *Poems*, 1933. Several collections.
Collected Poems, 1985.
Lost

30
NORMAN MacCAIG
Born 1910, Edinburgh. Royal High School, Edinburgh, and Edinburgh University.
Teacher. *Far Cry*, 1943. Numerous collections. *Collected Poems*, 1985.
A Truth in Two Halves

32
SORLEY MACLEAN [SOMHAIRLE MACGILL-EAIN]
Born 1911, Isle of Raasay, Skye. Portree High School and Edinburgh University.
Signal Corps World War II. Gaelic teacher.
Teacher.
17 Poems for 6d, in Gaelic, Lowland Scots and English, 1940. Several collections.
Spring Tide And Neap Tide: Selected Poems 1932-1972, 1977.
McIntyre and Ross

34
PAUL POTTS
Born 1911, Vancouver, Canada. Educated in Canada, Italy, and England.
Army Education Corps, World War II.
A Poet's Testament, foreword by Hugh MacDiarmid, 1940.
Instead Of A Sonnet, 1940, 1978. *Dante Called You Beatrice*, 1961.
Invitation To A Sacrament, 1973.
Note

36
ROY FULLER
Born 1912, Lancashire. Blackpool High School. Solicitor.
Director, Woolwich Equitable Building Society. Professor of Poetry, Oxford, 1968-73.
Poems, 1939. Numerous collections. *New And Collected Poems*, 1985.
Singing, 1977

38
LAWRENCE DURRELL
Born 1912, Julundur, India.
College of St Joseph, Darjeeling and St Edmund's School, Canterbury.
Novelist. *Quaint Fragment*, 1931. Numerous collections. *Collected Poems*, 1980.
Keepsake

40
GEORGE BARKER
Born 1913, Essex.
Marlborough Road School, Chelsea, and Regent Street Polytechnic.
Taught at universities in Japan, England, and America.
Thirty Preliminary Poems, 1933. Numerous collections. *Collected Poems*, 1987.
From 'At Thurgaton Church'

42
ELIZABETH SMART
1913-1986. Born Ottawa.
Hatfield Hall, Ontario, and London and California Universities.
By Grand Central Station I Sat Down and Wept, 1945. *A Bonus*, 1977.
In The Meantime, 1984.
A Warning

44
R.S.THOMAS
Born 1913, Glamorgan. University College, Bangor, and University of Wales.
Ordained as minister in the Church of Wales, 1936.
The Stones Of The Field, 1946. Numerous collections. *Selected Poems*, 1986.
Self-Portrait

46
ANNE RIDLER
Born 1912, Warwickshire.
Downe House School and King's College, London University.
Worked in publishing; playwright, literary editor.
Poems, 1939. Several collections. *Selected Poems*, 1961.
From 'Still-Life'

47
NORMAN NICHOLSON
Born 1914, Cumberland. Educated at local schools. Lecturer.
Five Rivers, 1944. Numerous collections. *Selected Poems*, 1982.
The Safe Side

48
C.H.SISSON
Born 1914, Bristol. Bristol, Berlin, Freiburg, and Paris Universities.
British Army Intelligence Corps, 1942-45. Civil servant; translator.
Poems, 1959. Several collections. *Collected Poems*, 1984.
From 'The Regrets'

50
LAURIE LEE
Born 1914, Gloucestershire. Slad Village School and Stroud Central School. Writer.
The Sun My Monument, 1944. Several collections. *Selected Poems*, 1983.
Words Asleep

52
GAVIN EWART
Born 1916, London. Wellington College and Christ's College, Cambridge.
Royal Artillery 1940-46. Advertising copywriter.
Poems And Songs, 1939. Numerous collections. *The Collected Ewart*, 1980.
Tennysonian Reflections at Barnes Bridge

54
DAVID GASCOYNE
Born 1916, Middlesex.
Salisbury Cathedral Choir School and Regent Street Polytechnic. Translator.
Roman Balcony, 1932. *A Short Survey Of Surrealism*, 1935. Several collections.
Collected Poems, 1965.
The Wall

56
CHARLES CAUSLEY
Born 1917, Cornwall. Launceston College and Peterborough Training College.
Royal Navy 1940-46.
Teacher. *Farewell, Aggie Weston*, 1951. Numerous collections. *Collected Poems*,
1975.
Night Before a Journey

58
W.S.GRAHAM
1918-1986. Born Renfrewshire, Scotland.
Greenock High School and Workers' Educational Association College, Edinburgh.
Engineer.
Cage Without Grievance, 1942. Several collections. *Collected Poems*, 1979.
Untidy Dreadful Table

60
JOHN HEATH-STUBBS
Born 1918, London. Bembridge School, Isle of Wight, and Queen's College, Oxford.
Taught at universities and colleges in Egypt, America, and England.
Wounded Thammuz, 1942. Numerous collections. *Selected Poems*, 1965.
Artorius, 1973.
A Crow in Bayswater

62
ELMA MITCHELL
Born 1919, Airdie, Scotland. Prior's Field School and Somerville College, Oxford.
Librarian.
The Poor Man In The Flesh, 1976. *The Human Cage*, 1979. *Furnished Rooms*, 1983.
Good Old Days

64
DAVID WRIGHT
Born 1920, Johannesburg.
St John's School, Johannesburg, Northampton School for the Deaf,
and Oriel College, Oxford.
Co-editor X magazine 1959-62. Literary editor.
Poems, 1949. Several collections.
To The Gods The Shades: New And Collected Poems, 1976.
Encounter in a Glass

66
MICHAEL HAMBURGER
Born 1924, Berlin. German, Scottish, English schools, and Christ Church, Oxford.
Army 1943-47. Taught at universities in Germany, England, and America. Translator.
Later Hogarth, 1945. Numerous collections. *Collected Poems*, 1984.
Cat

67
D.J.ENRIGHT
Born 1920, Warwickshire. Leamington College and Downing College, Cambridge.
Taught at universities in Europe and the Far East; publisher and reviewer.
Season Ticket, 1948. Numerous collections. *Collected Poems*, 1981.
The Word

68
EDWIN MORGAN
Born 1920 Glasgow. Glasgow High School and Glasgow University.
Professor of English at Glasgow University; translator.
The Vision Of Cathkin Braes, 1952. Numerous collections.
Poems Of Thirty Years, 1982.
The Poet

70
GEORGE MACKAY BROWN
Born 1921, Orkney, Scotland.
Stromness Academy, Newbattle Abbey College, and Edinburgh University.
Playwright, novelist, short story writer.
The Storm, 1954. Numerous collections. *Selected Poems*, 1977.
The Poet

72
KINGSLEY AMIS
Born 1922, London. City of London School and St John's College, Oxford.
Royal Corps of Signals 1942-45. Novelist.
Bright November, 1947. Several collections. *Collected Poems*, 1979.
Album-Leaf

74
DONALD DAVIE
Born 1922, Yorkshire.
Barnsley Grammar School and St Catharine's College, Cambridge.
Royal Navy 1941-46. Taught at universities in Ireland. England, and America.
Brides Of Reason, 1955. Numerous collections. *Collected Poems*, 1972.
Life Encompassed

76
PHILIP LARKIN
1922-1985. Born Warwickshire.
King Henry VIII School, Coventry, and St John's College, Oxford. Librarian.
The North Ship, 1945. *The Less Deceived*, 1955. *The Whitsun Weddings*, 1964.
High Windows, 1974.
A Study of Reading Habits

78
VERNON SCANNELL
Born 1922, Lincolnshire. Queen's Park School, Aylesbury, and University of Leeds.
Gordon Highlanders, 1941-45. Boxer; writer.
Graves & Resurrections, 1948. Numerous collections. *New & Collected Poems*, 1980.
The Men Who Wear My Clothes

80
DANNIE ABSE
Born 1923, Cardiff. St Illtyd's College, Cardiff, and University of South Wales. Physician.
After Every Green Thing, 1949. Numerous collections. *Collected Poems 1948-1976*, 1977.
Mysteries

82
PATRICIA BEER
Born 1924, Devon.
Exmouth Grammar School, Exeter University, and St Hugh's College, Oxford. Lecturer.
Loss of the Magyar and Other Poems, 1959. Numerous collections. *Selected Poems*, 1979.
Autobiography

84
JOHN WAIN
Born 1925, Staffordshire.
High School, Newcastle-under-Lyme, and St John's College, Oxford. Novelist and critic.
Professor of Poetry, Oxford, 1973-78.
Mixed Feelings, 1951. Numerous collections. *Poems 1949-1979*, 1981.
My Name

86
IAN HAMILTON FINLAY
Born 1925, Rousay, Orkney. Shepherd.
Copywriter. 'I'm a minor revolutionary,' he says, 'beginning with gardening.
The Dancers Inherit the Party, 1960. Numerous pamphlets and collections.
Works and areas constructed in parks in Europe.
Ian Hamilton Finlay: A Visual Primer, by Yves Abrioux, 1985.
From 'Monostichs de la Guerre de Petite-Sparte'

88
OLIVER BERNARD
Born 1925, Buckinghamshire. Westminster and London University.
RAF, 1943-47. Advertising copywriter, teacher, translator.
Country Matters, 1961. *Rimbaud*, 1962. *Apollinaire*, 1965, 1986. *Poems*, 1983.
that night

90
ELIZABETH JENNINGS
Born 1926, Lincolnshire. Oxford High School and St Anne's College, Oxford.
Worked in a library; advertising, publishing.
Poems, 1953. Numerous collections. *Collected Poems*, 1986.
I Feel

92
CHRISTOPHER LOGUE
Born 1926, Hampshire. Portsmouth Grammar School.
Army, 1944-48. Playwright, actor.
Wand & Quadrant, 1953. Numerous collections.
Ode To The Dodo, Poems 1953-78, 1981.
Last Night in London Airport

94
ANTHONY CRONIN
Born 1926, Co. Wexford, Eire. Blackrock College and University College, Dublin.
Novelist, broadcaster.
Poems, 1957. Several collections. *New and Selected Poems*, 1982.
Writing

95
RICHARD MURPHY
Born 1927, Co. Mayo, Eire.
King's School, Canterbury; Wellington; and Magdalen College, Oxford.
Taught at universities in England and America.
The Archaeology Of Love, 1955. Several collections. *Selected Poems*, 1979.
Moonshine

96
CHARLES TOMLINSON
Born 1927, Staffordshire. Longton High School and Queens' College, Cambridge.
Artist, translator; Reader in English, Bristol University.
Relations And Contraries, 1951. Numerous collections. *Collected Poems*, 1985.
Against Portraits

98
IAIN CRICHTON SMITH
Born 1928, Outer Hebrides. Stornoway School and University of Aberdeen.
Teacher, playwright, novelist.
The Long River, 1955. Numerous collections. *Selected Poems 1955-1980*, 1981.
Reflection

100
PETER PORTER
Born 1929, Brisbane, Australia. Church of England and Toowoomba Grammar Schools.
Journalist, advertising copywriter; broadcaster and critic.
Once Bitten, Twice Bitten, 1961. Numerous collections. *Collected Poems,* 1983.
From 'Returning'

102
JOHN MONTAGUE
Born 1929, Brooklyn, New York.
St Patrick's College, Armagh; University College, Dublin; Yale; and University of Iowa.
Film critic, journalist. Taught at universities in America and Ireland.
Forms Of Exile, 1958. Numerous collections. *Selected Poems,* 1982.
From 'The Well Dreams'

103
JON SILKIN
Born 1930, London. Wycliffe and Dulwich Colleges, and Leeds University.
Taught at universities in England, America, and Australia.
Founding co-editor *Stand* magazine, 1950. *The Portrait,* 1950.
Numerous collections. *Selected Poems,* 1980.
The chisel grows heavy

104
TED HUGHES
Born 1930, Yorkshire. Mexborough Grammar School and Pembroke College, Cambridge.
The Hawk In The Rain, 1957. Numerous collections. *Collected Poems 1957-1981,* 1982.
Poet Laureate 1984.
Famous Poet

106
ELAINE FEINSTEIN
Born 1930, Lancashire.
Wyggeston Grammar School, Leicester, and Newnham College, Cambridge.
Novelist, translator. *In A Green Eye,* 1966.
Several collections. *Some Unease and Angels: Selected Poems,* 1977.
Night Thoughts

108
ANTHONY THWAITE
Born 1930, Cheshire. Kingswood School, Bath, and Christ Church, Oxford.
Taught at universities in Japan, Libya, Kuwait.
Literary editor. *Poems,* 1953. Numerous collections. *Poems 1953-1983,* 1984.
By the Sluice

109
ALAN BROWNJOHN
Born 1931, London. Brockley County School and Merton College, Oxford.
Lecturer. *Travellers Alone,* 1954. Numerous collections.
Collected Poems 1952-1983, 1983.
Cure

110
P.J.KAVANAGH
Born 1931, Sussex. Douai School and Merton College, Oxford.
Lecturer, journalist. *One And One,* 1959. Numerous collections. *Selected Poems,* 1982.
Moving

112
PETER LEVI
Born 1931, Middlesex. Beaumont College, Berkshire, and Campion Hall, Oxford.
Jesuit priest 1965-77. Classical scholar, travel writer.
Professor of Poetry, Oxford, 1984.
Earthly Paradise, 1958. Numerous collections. *Collected Poems 1955-1975,* 1976.
The Greenhouse in October

114
GEOFFREY HILL
Born 1932, Worcestershire.
County High School, Bromsgrove, and Keble College, Oxford.
Fellow of Emmanuel College, Cambridge.
Poems, 1952. Several collections. *Collected Poems,* 1985.
Ovid in the Third Reich

116
GEORGE MacBETH
Born 1932, Lanarkshire. King Edward VII School, Sheffield, and New College, Oxford.
BBC producer. *A Form Of Words,* 1954. Numerous collections.
Collected Poems 1958-1970, 1971.
From 'The Renewal'

118
ADRIAN MITCHELL
Born 1932, London. Dauntsey's School, Wiltshire, and Christ Church, Oxford.
Journalist, playwright. *Poems,* 1955. Numerous collections.
For Beauty Douglas: Collected Poems 1953-1979, 1982.
Song in Space

119
FLEUR ADCOCK
Born 1934, Papakura, New Zealand.
Wellington Girls' College and Victoria University of Wellington.
Lecturer, librarian. *The Eye Of The Hurricane,* 1964. Several collections.
Selected Poems, 1983.
Foreigner

120
PETER REDGROVE AND PENELOPE SHUTTLE
Peter Redgrove born 1932, Surrey. Taunton School and Queens' College, Cambridge.
Scientific journalist, novelist.
The Collector, 1960. Numerous collections.
Sons Of My Skin: Selected Poems 1954-1974, 1975.
Several works in collaboration with poet and novelist Penelope Shuttle,
born 1947, Middlesex.
A Man and His Wife

122
ROGER McGOUGH
Born 1937, Liverpool. St Mary's College, Crosby, and Hull University.
Teacher, freelance writer and performer. *Watchwords,* 1969. Numerous collections.
Survivor

124
SEAMUS HEANEY
Born 1939, Castledawson, Londonderry.
St Columb's College, Derry, and Queen's University, Belfast.
Taught at universities in England, America, and Eire.
Eleven Poems, 1965. Numerous collections. *Selected Poems 1965-1975,* 1980.
From 'Exposure'

From
'The Turn of the World'
*(an old folk phrase for the time
between dark and dawn)*

In the turn of the world,
In the hour between dark and dawn,
Of what am I thinking?
No longer young now,
And having looked and heard so much,
I wonder –
Does one not wonder? –
Where we are going?
There is nothing to be sure of,
That is certain.

There is only the beauty of the world.
Not yet blighted,
And which may turn to anything.
Ah! in this little hour
Let us walk in the dawn
And wet our dew strings,
A countryman's phrase
In shepherd's language;
If it is not the false dawn
And a white ash is falling.

Sacheverell Sitwell

Complaint
After Psycho-Analysis

Now my days are all undone,
spirit sunken, girls forgone,
I shall weave in other mesh
than fading bone and flesh.

Into cold deserted mind
drag the relics of the blind;
and raise from wives none other sees
substantial families.

Hunt through woods of maidenhair
tangled in the shining air
the forms of ecstasies achieved –
not then believed.

O Unicorns and jewelled Birds
and trampling dappled moonlight Herds,
in icy glades now slain
with arrows bright as pain!

Leap, Moon, from the berg's pale womb!
Frail Bride, out of Earth's tomb!
The stars are ashen cold
beneath their gold.

Edgell Rickword

From Part V of
Briggflatts

Light lifts from the water.
Frost has put rowan down,
a russet blotch of bracken
tousled about the trunk.
Bleached sky. Cirrus
reflects sun that has left
nothing to badger eyes.

Wet Evening in April

The birds sang in the wet trees
And as I listened to them it was a hundred years from now
And I was dead and someone else was listening to them.
But I was glad I had recorded for him
   The melancholy.

Patrick Kavanagh

Thank You

What's the good of mourning
This passing of poets?
Be glad they have lived,

Intermittently sozzled with words,
Unslurred, on this side and that side
Of the Absurd.

Geoffrey Grigson

The Last Laugh

I made hay while the sun shone.
   My work sold.
Now, if the harvest is over
   And the world cold,
Give me the bonus of laughter
   As I lose hold.

John Betjeman

From

Autumn on Nan-Yueh

(With the exiled universities of Peking)

I said I wouldn't fly again
    For quite a bit. I did not know.
Even in breathing tempest-tossed,
    Scattering to winnow and to sow,
With convolutions for a brain,
    Man moves, and we have got to go.
Claiming no heavy personal cost
    I feel the poem would be slow
Furtively finished on the plain.
    We have had the autumn here. But oh
That lovely balcony is lost
    Just as the mountains take the snow.
The soldiers will come here and train.
    The streams will chatter as they flow.

William Empson.

Coming Into Your Room

Coming into your room I spoke your name,
Paused in the doorway, but no answer came.

Sun through the window slanted dusty down
On bookshelves patterned crimson, gold and brown,
And framed the roses, with their August air
Of heart and haven, in a burning square,
Creeping to light your scarf that lay beside
My opened letter, pens, a Spanish guide.

So sharply then I felt our summer there,
Reproach, a bubble broken, left despair;
It seemed no sense that phrases could offend,
No reason valid for a scribbled end;
If you'd but come, I could have made it plain,
There, in the silence; but I stayed in vain.

Time's tower bells outside repeating four,
Their empty epilogue, I closed the door.

John Lehmann

Afternoon Sunlight Plays

Afternoon sunlight plays
Through trailing leaves I cannot see,
Stirred by a little wind that mixes light and leaf
To filter their quiet pattern on my floor.
Not real, Plato said, the shadowy dancers,
Imponderable,
Somewhere beyond, the light; but I am old,
Content with these shadows of shadows that visit me,
Present unsummoned, gone without stir.

So angels, it may be.

Kathleen Raine.

Lost

Horizontal on amber air, three boughs of green
Lift slotted sleeves. Beyond them, the house glows.
Straight mouldings delineate tall windows.
Glass panes hold the balance between
Garden mirrored and interior darkly seen.

That cracked stucco wall seems the harsh rind
Of a fruit, guarding sweetness I savour:
My dreams, like teeth, penetrate the flavour
Of its honeyed withheld life behind
Whose taste once entered me, body and mind.

Against that wall my hungry memories press
To reach back to the time that was my heart.
One room, my heart, holds a girl with lips apart
Watching a child, starry in nakedness.
Her gaze covers him like a fleecy dress.

This is that room where the world was most precious.
Jewelled silence in their eyes collects
Light that each from each all day reflects.
Here life and furniture are gracious,
All times and places outside here, atrocious.

My spirit, strayed in wars abroad, seems ghost
Gazing through gales and clay on his warm past.
Now from my empty everywhere I cast
Unseen unseeing glances through time lost
Back to that sole room where life was life most.

Stephen Spender

A Truth in Two Halves

A bulge of light sits on that shelf
As though the idea of a jar
Had thickened and become a self.

Half self, half light. I stare and can't
Be easy with what seems at once
Visitor and visitant.

I know the light won't take it back,
Dissolving it before my eyes.
– Yet turn the light out. In the black

Cube of a room, I hold the jar
Like a fish under water and
My world is not where my hands are.

Norman MacCaig

McIntyre and Ross

Not different the fate of bards
from those who do not work with words.
Luck was on McIntyre's side
but William Ross was edified
with pain and consumption till he died.

Sorley MacLean

Mac an T-saoir is ros

Chan eil freasdal nam bàrd
dealaichte bho fhreasdal chàich:
bha 'm fortan le Donnchadh Bàn
is fhuair Uilleam Ros a shàth
de'n àmhghar, de'n chaitheamh 's de'n bhàs.

Somhairle MacGill-Eain

Note

My dreams
Watching me said
One to the other
This life has let us down.

Paul Potts

Singing, 1977

For most of my life, no need to wear specs.
Now I look over them at meetings
With the aplomb of a rotten actor,
Push them around my bumf when spouting,
Needlessly checking the earpieces' hinges.
Of all my portraits I say: poor likeness.
'Colonel (Retired)' or 'Disgusted' stares out,
Doomed to expire of apoplexy;
Whitening moustache, jaw-line sagging.
Like a woman, I think: I've lost my looks.
Reactionary views, advanced mostly
To raise a laugh – taken as gospel!

Keepsake

To increase your hold
Relax your grip,
Exploit the slip twixt
Cup and lip.

Enjoy and bid and let it grow,
Superior sense of vertigo,
The adepts' sixth infernal sense
Spells passionate indifference,
So by the racing pulse express
A discipline of laziness.

To increase your scope
Relax your hold
Not wish nor hope
One second old
The key to open all the locks
Of this insidious paradox,
Not wish nor hope one second old
So all that glitters may be gold.

Lawrence Durrell

From
At Thurgarton Church

I enter and find I stand
in a great barn, bleak and bare;
like ice the winter ghosts and
the white walls gleam and flare
and flame as the sun drops low.

I know as I leave I shall pass
where Thurgarton's dead lie
at those old stones in the grass
under the cold moon's eye.
I see the old bones glow.

I hear the old bone in me cry
and the dying spirit call:
I have forfeited all
and once and for all must die
and this is all that I know.

For now in a wild way we
know that Justice is served
and that we die in the clay we
dread, desired and deserved,
awaiting no judgement day.

George Barker

A Warning

This old woman
Waddles towards love,
Becomes human,
But the Muse does not approve.

This going flesh
Is loved and is forgiven
By the generous
But houses a daemon.

Hullo, my dear, sit down,
I'll soothe your pain;
I've known what you've known,
But won't again,

Though passion is not gone,
Merely contracted
Into a last-ditch weapon,
A word not dead,

A mine unexploded,
And not safe
To have near the playground
Of innocent life.

Keep clear of this frail
Old harmless person:
Sixty year's fuel
Of aimed frustration

Could shatter the calm
And scald the soul
And love fall like napalm
Over the school.

Elizabeth Smart

Self-Portrait

That resigned look! Here I am,
it says; fifty-nine,
balding, shirking the challenge
of the young girls. Time running out
now, and the soul
unfinished. And the heart knows
this is not the portrait
it posed for. Keep the lips
firm; too many disappointments
have turned the mouth down
at the corners. There is no surgery
can mend those lines; cruelly
the light fingers them and the mind
winces. All that skill,
life, on the carving
of the curved nostril and to no end
but disgust. The hurrying eyes
pause, waiting for an outdistanced
gladness to overtake them.

R. S Thomas

From

Still Life

Night passed and the fog froze;
The moon passed, but not her silence: when the sun rose,
Rigid and mute his world, a fist
Clenched and contracted, every branch and plant encased
In quartz and scored with siliceous white –
A world struck solid and paralysed with light.

Absolute calm, absolute silence
Both to the eye and ear, but the skin feels violence,
Feels a pain whose origin is lost:
Impotent burning of the sun, or grip of the deaf-mute frost.

Anne Ridler

The Safe Side

'It's better to be on the safe side,' my father used to say,
Picking up an umbrella when there was scarcely a cloud in the wide
Shop-window of the sky. Now, wearing his greyness, I
Lean on my wordy counter, totting up dots and commas,
Expounding that much and this much if not exactly twice
Yet rather more than once – to be on the safe side.

From

The Regrets

Beware of age.
For I have learned
An old man should
Be kept in chains.
He is a gentle
Psychopath;
The passion that
He had is dead.
His youthful walk
And grey moustache
Conceal a heart
Which cannot feel.
The courtesy
Which he expends
Is poison to
His younger friends.
His virtues are
A kind of shell
To keep him cosy
In his skull.
I tell you mark
This leper well
And send him forward
With a bell.

Words Asleep

Now I am still and spent
and lie in a whited sepulchre
breathing dead

but there will be
no lifting of the damp swathes
no return of blood
no rolling away the stone

till the cocks carve sharp
gold scars in the morning
and carry the stirring sun
and early dust to my ears.

Andalucia

Laurie Lee

Tennysonian Reflections
at Barnes Bridge

The river flows before my door,
Sad with sea-gulls, mute with mud
Past Hammersmith and Castelnau,
And strung with barges at the flood.
Pink rowing girls by eight and four
Gently stroke the tide of blood.

A railway runs from side to side
And trains clank over on the hour.
The rowers strain and stretch and slide,
Hair like chrysanthemums, the flower
Of girlhood not yet opened wide,
Each happy in her virgin power.

The dying sun, the dying day
With sunlight charms suburban reaches,
The hackneyed river flows away,
And Time runs too, experience teaches,
Nor for the boring bard will stay
Or rowing girls as fresh as peaches.

Gavin Ewart

The Wall

At first my territory was a Wood:
Tanglewood, tattering tendrils, trees
Whose Grimm's-tale shadow terrified but made
A place to hide in: among traps and towers
The path I kept to had free right-of-way.

But centred later round an ambushed Well,
Reputed bottomless; and night and day
My gaze hung in the depths beneath the real
And sought the secret source of nothingness;
Until I tired of its Circean spell.

Returning to the narrow onward road
I find it leads me only to the Wall
Of Interdiction. But if my despair
Is strong enough, my spirit truly hard,
No wall shall break my will: To persevere.

David Gascoyne

Night Before a Journey

Books on the printed wall
Withhold their speech;
Pencil and paper and pen
Move out of reach.

The longcase clock in the hall
Winds carefully down.
No matter, says the house-ghost.
He is already gone.

A flower fallen on the shelf,
The stain of moon, of sun,
A wine-glass forgotten –
All await the return.

Nothing in the stopped house
Shall unbalance the air.
There is one, says the house-ghost,
Who is always here.

Patiently watching, waiting,
Moving from room to stilled room,
Light as breath, clear as light.
This, too, is his home.

When shall we meet, the stranger
And I, one with another?
When you leave for the last time,
Says the house-ghost. And together.

Untidy Dreadful Table

Lying with no love on the paper
Between the typing hammers I spied
Myself with looking eyes looking
Down to cover me with words.

I won't have it. I know the night
Is late here sitting at my table,
But I am not a boy running
The hide and seeking streets.

I am getting on. My table now
Shuffles its papers out of reach
With last year's letters going yellow
From looking out of the window.

I sit here late and I hammer myself
On to the other side of the paper.
There I jump through all surprises.
The reader and I are making faces.

I am not complaining. Some of the faces
I see are interesting indeed.
Take your own, for example, a fine
Grimace of vessels over the bone.

Of course I see you backwards covered
With words backwards from the other side.
I must tackle my dreadful table
And go on the hide and seeking hill.

W S Graham

A Crow in Bayswater

A carrion crow flew over Bayswater –
Dews of morning distilled on his dark wings.

Shadows of night retired – the ghost
Of Peter Rachman, pursued
By phantom Alsatian dogs,
Scurried down St Stephen's Gardens.

He sailed over All Saints Church, and Father Clark
Unlocking the door for Anglican Eucharist;

Over spilling dustbins, where
Warfarin-resistant mice
Licked the insides of empty soup-cans,
Worried
Potato peelings, stale sliced bread.

'Cark!' said the crow, a raucous croak – to me
The stern music of freedom –

'I will go to Kensington Gardens;
Down by the Round Pond.
New-hatched ducklings are out:
We'll scrag a couple for breakfast.'

John Heath-Stubbs

Good Old Days

My neck, where love ran
Just under the skin
Is now an old rickety ladder to the brain.

My breasts, a full delight
For child and man,
The setting
To carry rival jewels,
Dangle now untidy,
Unharvested, over-ripe.

The wishbone of my legs
Has changed their wishes' destination,
Shin repeats to shin,
Welcome, death, you may come in.

I should be cheerless
As a crow in winter fields
When the light is going

But up here, at the top of the spine, behind the eyes,
Curtained a little, but not blind,
Sits a young and laughing mind
Wondering which part of me is telling lies.

Elma Mitchell.

Encounter in a Glass

Skin coarse, bird-shotted nose, the flesh loose,
Almost a hammock underneath the chin;
Eyebrows en brosse – a zareba, that one –
A sprout of hair in earhole and nostril,
Lines traversing like mountain trods the forehead –
I almost wondered who the fellow was.

I knew him well enough, the non-stranger,
Yet was – as, despite a remembered face,
One can't identify some familiar
Acquaintance in an unaccustomed place -
About to make the oddest of faux pas:
To offer him my seat, and call him sir.

David Wright

Cat

Unfussy lodger, she knows what she wants and gets it:
Food, cushions, fires, the run of the garden.
I, her night porter in the small hours
Don't bother to grumble, grimly let her in.
To that coldness she purrs assent,
Eats her fill and outwits me,
Plays hide and seek in the dark house.

Only at times, by chance meeting the gaze
Of her amber eyes that can rest on me
As on a beech-bole, on bracken or meadow grass
I'm moved to celebrate the years between us,
The farness and the nearness:
My fingers graze her head.
To that fondness she purrs assent.

Michael Hamburger

The Word

The sage said: We are all books
In the great Library of God.
(He was a bookish person.)

One asked: Does He ever
Take us out?
We spend our years as a tale that is told.

The sage said: His will be done
In the Library as it is Elsewhere.

One asked: But perhaps
He is only interested in first editions,
Not in reprints, abridgements, strip cartoon
Or other adaptations?

The sage said: His love speaks volumes.
He is a speed reader. He is no respecter
Of Bestseller lists.
He suffers the little magazines to come unto Him.

Some hoped their jackets would be clean
And well pressed when the call was heard,
Their loins girded about and their lights burning.

God thought: I wrote all the books,
Now they expect Me to read them.

The Poet

The poet shrieks getting
waiting out of his system
when the little wringing hands
of a valetudinary muse
fuse to one white claw.

He shivers as he bleeds.
Eagle country, winds
and pines, the lower air
thick with dying leaves,
a gleam of flooded fields.
Whatever it is that will
not wait, he still half waits
to find, half sees, feels
wholly as the unrelenting
hook hangs him higher
and higher and something like
wings or the single wing
of a great craft shadows
and flashes alternately past
the sun of that country.
At the right moment the claw
retracts, and his one clear cry
falls to the earth before him,
winding down like a song.

The Poet

Therefore he no more troubled the pool of silence
But put on mask and cloak,
Strung a guitar
And moved among the folk.
Dancing they cried,
'Ah, how our sober islands
Are gay again, since this blind lyrical tramp
Invaded the Fair!'

Under the last dead lamp
When all the dancers and masks had gone inside
His cold stare
Returned to its true task, interrogation of silence.

George Mackay Brown

Album-Leaf

A photograph can't speak or move its face,
And so the ones we find in frames and books
Seem like the real faces of you and me
Now we no longer like each other's looks;
Self-regard cramps them to stupidity;
Their history of movement leaves no trace.

And this is scarcely queer, but it was queer
That once, during a well-composed embrace,
Something disturbed that studio veneer;
The self-regard of each got holed right through.
Or else we wished it had, or seemed to.

Kingsley Amis

Life Encompassed

How often I have said,
'This will never do,'
Of ways of feeling that now
I trust in, and pursue!

Do traverses tramped in the past,
My own, criss-crossed as I forge
Across from another quarter
Speak of a life encompassed?

Well, life is not research.
No one asks you to map the terrain,
Only to get across it
In new ways, time and again.

How many such, even now,
I dismiss out of hand
As not to my purpose, not
Unknown, just unexamined.

A Study of
Reading Habits

When getting my nose in a book
Cured most things short of school,
It was worth ruining my eyes
To know I could still keep cool,
And deal out the old right hook
To dirty dogs twice my size.

Later, with inch-thick specs,
Evil was just my lark:
Me and my cloak and fangs
Had ripping times in the dark.
The women I clubbed with sex!
I broke them up like meringues.

Don't read much now: the dude
Who lets the girl down before
The hero arrives, the chap
Who's yellow and keeps the store,
Seem far too familiar. Get stewed:
Books are a load of crap.

The Men Who Wear My Clothes

Sleepless I lay last night and watched the slow
    Procession of the men who wear my clothes:
First, the grey man with bloodshot eyes and sly
    Gestures miming what he loves and loathes.

Next came the cheery knocker-back of pints,
    The beery joker, never far from tears,
Whose loud and public vanity acquaints
    The careful watcher with his private fears.

And then I saw the neat mouthed gentle man
    Defer politely, listen to the lies,
Smile at the tedious tale and gaze upon
    The little mirrors in the speaker's eyes.

The men who wear my clothes walked past my bed
    And all of them looked tired and rather old;
I felt a chip of ice melt in my blood.
    Naked I lay last night, and very cold.

Vernon Scannell

Mysteries

At night, I do not know who I am
when I dream, when I am sleeping.

Awakened, I hold my breath and listen:
a thumbnail scratches the other side of the wall.

At midday, I enter a sunlit room
to observe the lamplight on for no reason.

I should know by now that few octaves can be
    heard
that a vision dies from being too long stared at;

that the whole of recorded history even
is but a little gossip in a great silence;

that a magnesium flash cannot illumine,
for one single moment, the invisible.

I do not complain. I start with the visible
and am startled by the visible.

Dannie Abse

Autobiography

I sailed through many waters,
Cold following warm because I moved
Though Arctic and equator were steady.

Harbours sank as I discarded them,
Landmarks melted into the sky
When I needed them no longer.

I left behind all weathers.
I passed dolphins, flying-fish and seagulls
That are ships in their own stories.

Patricia Beer

My Name

*(If I lived in a culture whose poets take bardic Names,
I would choose to be called Flying-fish.)*

Flying-fish loves the salt kiss of brine:
Flying-fish loves the leap into slanting air.

Flying-fish loves the bottle-green of the depths:
his soul expands in the diminishing light.

Flying-fish fears the dry smack of a deck-landing:
Flying-fish fears the ring of grinning captors.

Flying-fish fears the slyness of net and trawl,
he grieves for his brothers who thrash in that stricture.

Flying-fish offers his sperm to the smooth scales of
   a mate:
he loves to come close amid the vastness of ocean.

Flying-fish fears the bleep of sonic detectors:
to escape technology, he flashes through air and foam.

Flying-fish is nourished by the marrow of colours
a rainbow fattens him like a wedding-breakfast.

Flying-fish does not fear death.
Night is friendly to him, and death is night:

calm night on the ocean, with uncountable stars,
and fragrances blowing off the islands.

When the time comes, he will accept night:
meanwhile each morning and evening he splashes and glides,

in search of more life, singing in water-language:
MORE, MORE, MORE, ALWAYS LET THERE BE MORE!

John Wain

From
Monostichs de la Guerre
de Petite-Sparte

Classical warfare
The capital fell to an enemy column.

Classical biography
No man is a hero to his valley.

Ian Hamilton Finlay

that night

crossing the bridge I met my ghost
is it you he said I've waited for
hours well here I am at last
said I where have you been not far
just down the river to the pub

what did you do he asked we talked
well then did you learn something new
now never mind I said we walked
down the long dyke the moon a few
nights old shone white black water lapped

my solitude is like that ghost
that sometimes I call loneliness
and can't go home to answer though
all he asks is for the best
but we were not bad friends that night

Oliver Bernard

I Feel

I feel I could be turned to ice
If this goes on, if this goes on.
I feel I could be buried twice
And still the death not yet be done.

I feel I could be turned to fire
If there can be no end to this.
I know within me such desire
No kiss could satisfy, no kiss.

I feel I could be turned to stone,
A solid block not carved at all,
Because I feel so much alone.
I could be grave-stone or a wall.

But better to be turned to earth
Where other things at least can grow.
I could be than a part of birth,
Passive, not knowing how to know.

Elizabeth Jennings

Last Night
In London Airport

Last night in London Airport
I saw a wooden bin
labelled **UNWANTED LITERATURE**
IS TO BE PLACED HEREIN.

So I wrote a poem
and popped it in.

Christopher Logue

Writing

Our happiness is easily wronged by speech,
Being complete like silence, globed like summer,
Without extension in regret or wish.
Outside that sky are all our past and future.

So in those moments when we can imagine
The almost perfect, nearly true, we keep
The words away from it, content with knowledge,
Naming it only as we fall asleep.

In suffering we call out for another,
Describing with a desperate precision.
We must be sure that this is how all suffer

Or be alone forever with the pain.
And all our search for words is one assertion:
'You would forgive me if I could explain.'

Moonshine

To think
I must be alone:
To love
We must be together.

I think I love you
When I'm alone
More than I think of you
When we're together.

I cannot think
Without loving
Or love
Without thinking.

Alone I love
To think of us together:
Together I think
I'd love to be alone.

Richard Murphy

Against Portraits

How, beyond all foresight
or intention, light
plays with a face
whose features play with light:

frame on gilded frame,
ancestor on ancestor,
the gallery is filled
with more certainty than we can bear:

if there must be
an art of portraiture,
let it show us ourselves as we
break from the image of what we are:

the animation of speech, and then
the eyes eluding
that which, once spoken,
seems too specific, too concluding:

or, entering a sudden slant
of brightness, between dark and gold,
a face half-hesitant,
face at a threshold:

Charles Tomlinson

Reflection

In the oval mirror
I see my face reflected.

'Hullo' I say to the mirror
'you're wearing a fine suit.

You're wearing a nice wristwatch
and shoes that are well polished.

Where are you going today?
Can I come with you?'

Iain Crichton Smith

From

Returning

It is time to recompose the face
Into a serious map, the children now
Envied creatures across a room, the case
Being settled for the present. Home is
The veteran of the adjectival run,
His images intact. He has learned how
To live another day and wakes, ringed
By the golden wallpaper of the sun.

Peter Porter

From

The Well Dreams

People are different.
They live outside, insist
in their world of agitation.
A man comes by himself,
singing or in silence,
and hauls up his bucket slowly –
an act of meditation –
or jerks it up angrily,
like lifting a skin,
sweeping a circle
right through his own reflection.

The chisel grows heavy

The chisel grows heavy, fewer words
would lighten the hands; and to keep
him who wanders this hard ground
like scurf, scurf the size of leaves,
or who grazes the mild squares
of London, is unseemly.

So who is this?
Earth's fingers revolve earth. Those
who search
will pass through me.

Famous Poet

Stare at the monster: remark
How difficult it is to define just what
Amounts to monstrosity in that
Very ordinary appearance. Neither thin nor fat,
    Hair between light and dark,

And the general air
Of an apprentice – say, an apprentice house-
Painter amid an assembly of famous
Architects: the demeanour is of mouse,
    Yet is he monster.

First scrutinize those eyes
For the spark, the effulgence: nothing. Nothing there
But the haggard stony exhaustion of a near-
Finished variety artist. He slumps in his chair
    Like a badly hurt man, half life-size.

Is it his dreg-boozed inner demon
Still tankarding from tissue and follicle
The vital fire, the spirit electrical
That puts the gloss on a normal hearty male?
    Or is it women?

The truth – bring it on
With black drapery, drums and funeral tread
Like a great man's coffin – no, no, he is not dead
But in this truth surely half-buried:
    Once, the humiliation

Of youth and obscurity,
The autoclave of heady ambition trapped,
The fermenting of the yeasty heart stopped –
Burst with such pyrotechnics the dull world gaped
    And "Repeat that!" still they cry.

But all his efforts to concoct
The old heroic bang from their money and praise
From the parent's pointing finger and the child's amaze
Even from the burning of his wreathed bays,
    Have left him wrecked: wrecked,

And monstrous, so,
As a Stegosaurus, a lumbering obsolete
Arsenal of gigantic horn and plate
From a time when half the world still burned, set
    To blink behind bars at the zoo.

Ted Hughes

Night thoughts

Uncurtained, my long room floats on
   darkness, moored in rain,
my shelves of orange skillets
   lie out in the black grass.
Tonight I can already taste
   the wet soil of their ghosts.
And my spirit looks through the glass:
   I cannot hold on for ever.

No tenure, in garden trees, I
   hang like a leaf, and stare
at cartilaginous shapes
   my shadow their visitor.
And words cannot brazen it out.
   Nothing can hold for ever.

Elaine Feinstein

By the Sluice

It pulses like a skin, at dusk
Is shaken like dusty silk. The current moves
But takes its impetus and gathers speed
Only beyond the sluice-gate. Here, the faint
Shudders, the morse of water almost trapped,
Perform half mesmerised, half dying too.

Yet are not dying: those trembling dots, those small
Reverberations, rise from what is hidden –
Scatters of minnows, nervous hair-triggered fry –
Grasping at sustenance, grabbing at what is given,
Submerged ferocities, brute delicacies.

What have I hidden here, or let go, lost,
With less to come than's gone, and so much gone?
Under the gate the river slams its door.

Cure

The rash fading out fades in
This annealed body, a photoprint
Coming solidly and slowly into focus
Out of a hot pink haze. Therefore a man
Is walking towards you into his daytime

And stopping, in bright mid-stride. By now
He has sharpened into something utterly
Steady, in a self-knowledge: the scare
May never return today to repossess
His sunlight. He is free of his own mists.

Moving

There is a perfect
socket at the centre
in whose groove
our lives would move
                      effortlessly.
Some physical men
have sometimes found it;
great games-players
on their day:
Garfield Sobers;
what do the others
find so difficult?
See, his simpleness!

In happiness
I spread my arms.
Dark
fish move in their shadow.

And I rejoice
my life as it should be –
moving towards
                    effortfully
its centre –
a kind of
happy nightmare.

P. J. Kavanagh

The Greenhouse in October

Relaxing among hanging plants
I notice a cold light which slants
in through the panes from brittle air
(gardens are places for despair)
putting a butterfly to sleep,
textures rough, colours deep,
and trails of leaf transmute their height
through falls more fugitive than flight,
vague-fingered things: yet out of these
I take my words and my wishes.

Peter Levi

Ovid in the Third Reich

non peccat, quaecumque potest peccasse negare,
solaque famosam culpa professa facit.
(AMORES, III, XIV)

I love my work and my children. God
Is distant, difficult. Things happen.
Too near the ancient troughs of blood
Innocence is no earthly weapon.

I have learned one thing: not to look down
So much upon the damned. They, in their sphere,
Harmonize strangely with the divine
Love. I, in mine, celebrate the love-choir.

Geoffrey Hill

From

The Renewal

I needed somewhere with a flirt of grace
To match your fervour for long acreage.
I found it, here at Oby. Naked space

Over the cornfields, and the next-door farm,
Contracts to an oasis with great trees
That North-East winds can ravage in their rage

And leave still rooted and serene. In these
I feel the sweep of beech-wood, like an arm,
And something deeper, in our copper beech.

That brings a birth-right in its massive reach,
A sense of giant time. Seeing it blaze
In widespread feathering, I feel the past,

The creek of longships on the Caister shore,
The swing of mills beside the easy broads,
And something closer, groping slow, at last,

The pleasant rectors, knocking croquet balls.

Song in Space

When man first flew beyond the sky
He looked back into the world's blue eye.
Man said: What makes your eye so blue?
Earth said: The tears in the oceans do.
Why are the seas so full of tears?
Because I've wept so many thousand years.
Why do you weep as you dance through a space?
Because I am the Mother of the Human Race.

Adrian Mitchell

Foreigner

These winds bully me:

I am to lie down in a ditch
quiet under the thrashing nettles
and pull the mud up to my chin.

Not that I would submit so
to one voice only;
but by the voices of these several winds
merged into a flowing fringe of tones
that swirl and comb over the hills
I am compelled.

I shall lie sound-proofed in the mud,
a huge caddis-fly larva,
a face floating upon Egyptian unguents
in a runnel at the bottom of England.

A Man and his Wife

I heard a man and his wife
discussing fire:
He said, how long
will you watch the flames?
She said, until the windmills
blaze for me
Who is in the room?
Her coat weeps
His hands hunt
The winter bride is afraid
and longs for the freedom of the fire
She refuses to answer his question
Her hair burns black
The candle is born

Peter Redgrove   *Penelope Shuttle*

Survivor

Everyday
I think about dying.
About disease, starvation,
violence, terrorism, war,
the end of the world.

It helps
keep my mind off things.

Roger McGough

From
Exposure

Rain comes down through the alders,
Its low conducive voices
Mutter about let-downs and erosions
And yet each drop recalls

The diamond absolutes.
I am neither internee nor informer;
An inner émigré, grown long-haired
And thoughtful; a wood-kerne

Escaped from the massacre,
Taking protective colouring
From bole and bark, feeling
Every wind that blows;

Who, blowing up these sparks
For their meagre heat, have missed
The once-in-a-lifetime portent,
The comet's pulsing rose.

Seamus Heaney

ACKNOWLEDGEMENTS

Dannie Abse: 'Mysteries'
from *Funland and Other Poems*, Hutchinson, 1973,
copyright © Dannie Abse.
Reprinted by permission of Anthony Sheil Associates Ltd.
Fleur Adcock : 'Foreigner'
copyright © Fleur Adcock 1979;
from Fleur Adcock's *Selected Poems*, 1983.
Reprinted by permission of Oxford University Press.
Kingsley Amis: 'Album-Leaf'
from *A Case of Samples*, Hutchinson,
copyright © Kingsley Amis 1956.
Reprinted by permission of Century Hutchinson Ltd,
and Jonathan Clowes Ltd, London,
on behalf of Kingsley Amis.
George Barker: 'At Thurgarton Church'
from *Poems of Places and People* by George Barker, 1971.
Reprinted by permission of Faber and Faber Ltd,
and John Johnson Ltd.
Patricia Beer: 'Autobiography' from *The Estuary*, Macmillan, 1971.
Reprinted by permission of the author.
Oliver Bernard: 'that night'
from *Country Matters*, Putnam, 1961.
Reprinted by permission of the author.
John Betjeman: 'The Last Laugh'
from John Betjeman's *Collected Poems*,
John Murray, 1979.
Reprinted by permission of John Murray.
Alan Brownjohn: 'Cure'
copyright © Alan Brownjohn 1986.
Printed by permission of the author.
Basil Bunting: from Part V of *Briggflatts*
copyright © Basil Bunting 1978;
from Basil Bunting's *Collected Poems*, 1978.
Reprinted by permission of Oxford University Press.
Charles Causley: 'Night Before a Journey'
from *Secret Destinations*, Macmillan, 1984.
Reprinted by permission of David Higham Associates Ltd.
Anthony Cronin: 'Writing'
from *New and Selected Poems*, Carcanet, 1982.
Reprinted by permission of the publishers.
Donald Davie: 'Life Encompassed'
from *Events and Wisdoms*, Routledge and Kegan Paul, 1964.
Reprinted by permission of the author.
Lawrence Durrell: 'Keepsake'
from *Collected Poems 1931-1974* by Lawrence Durrell
copyright © 1980 by Lawrence Durrell.
Reprinted by permission of Faber and Faber Ltd and Viking Penguin Inc.
D.J.Enright: 'The Word'
from D.J.Enright's *Collected Poems*, Oxford University Press, 1981.
Reprinted by permission of Watson, Little Ltd.
William Empson: 'Autumn On Nan-Yueh'
from *The Gathering Storm*, The Hogarth Press, 1940.
Reprinted by permission of the author's estate and Chatto & Windus.
Gavin Ewart: 'Tennysonian Reflections at Barnes Bridge'
from *Londoners* by Gavin Ewart, Heinemann, 1964.
Reprinted by permission of William Heinemann Ltd.
Elaine Feinstein: 'Night Thoughts'
from *The Celebrants*, Hutchinson, 1973.
Reprinted by permission of Century Hutchinson and Olwyn Hughes Literary Agency.
Ian Hamilton Finlay:
from 'Monostichs de la Guerre de Petite-Sparte'
copyright © Ian Hamilton Finlay 1986.
Reprinted by permission of the author.
Roy Fuller: 'Singing, 1977'
from *New and Collected Poems*, Secker & Warburg, 1985.
Reprinted by permission of Martin Secker & Warburg Ltd.
David Gascoyne: 'The Wall'
copyright © Oxford University Press, 1965;
from David Gascoyne's *Collected Poems*
edited by Robin Skelton, 1965.
Reprinted by permission of Oxford University Press.
W.S.Graham: 'Untidy Dreadful Table'
from *Implements in their Places*, Faber and Faber, 1977.
Reprinted by permission of Mrs Nessie Graham.
Geoffrey Grigson: 'Thank You'
from *The Cornish Dancer*, Secker & Warburg, 1982.
Reprinted by permission of Martin Secker & Warburg Ltd.
Michael Hamburger: 'Cat'
from *Collected Poems*, Carcanet Press, 1984.
Reprinted by permission of the author and publishers.

Seamus Heaney:
from 'Exposure' from *North* by Seamus Heaney, Faber and Faber, 1975.
Reprinted by permission of Faber and Faber Ltd; and from *Poems 1965-1975*,
copyright © 1966, 1969, 1972, 1975, 1980 by Seamus Heaney.
Reprinted by permission of Farrar, Straus & Giroux, Inc.
John Heath-Stubbs: 'A Crow in Bayswater'
from *The Watchman's Flute*, Carcanet Press, 1978.
Reprinted by permission of David Higham Associates Ltd.
Geoffrey Hill: 'Ovid in the Third Reich'
from *King Log*, André Deutsch, 1968.
Reprinted by permission of André Deutsch Ltd.
Ted Hughes: 'Famous Poet' from *Hawk in the Rain* by Ted Hughes,
Faber and Faber, 1957.
Reprinted by permission of Faber and Faber Ltd and Harper and Row, Publishers, Inc.
Elizabeth Jennings: 'I Feel'
from *Growing Points*, Carcanet Press, 1975.
Reprinted by permission of David Higham Associates Ltd.
Patrick Kavanagh: 'Wet Evening in April'
from *Collected Poems*, Macgibbon & Kee, 1964.
Reprinted by permission of Martin Brian & O'Keeffe Ltd.
P.J.Kavanagh: 'Moving'
from *On the Way to the Depot*,
Chatto & Windus/The Hogarth Press, 1968.
Reprinted by permission of the author and Chatto & Windus.
Philip Larkin: 'A Study of Reading Habits'
from *The Whitsun Weddings* by Philip Larkin, 1964.
Reprinted by permission of Faber and Faber Ltd.
Laurie Lee: 'Words Asleep' from
Selected Poems, André Deutsch, 1983.
Reprinted by permission of André Deutsch Ltd.
Peter Levi: 'The Greenhouse in October'
from *Water, Rock, and Sand*, André Deutsch, 1962.
Reprinted by permission of André Deutsch Ltd.
John Lehmann: 'Coming into Your Room'
from *The Age of the Dragon*, Longmans, 1951.
Reprinted by permission of David Higham Associates Ltd.
Christopher Logue: 'Last Night in London Airport'
from *Ode To The Dodo, Poems 1953-1978*
available from Turret Books, 42 Lamb's Conduit Street, London WC1N 3 LJ.
George Macbeth: from 'The Renewal'
from *Poems from Oby*, Secker & Warburg, 1982.
Reprinted by permission of Martin Secker & Warburg Ltd and the author.
Norman MacCaig: 'A Truth in Two Halves'
from *The White Bird*, Chatto & Windus/The Hogarth Press, 1973.
Reprinted by permission of the author and Chatto & Windus.
Roger McGough: 'Survivor'
from *Holiday on Death Row*, Jonathan Cape, 1979.
Reprinted by permission of the publisher and A.D.Peters & Co. Ltd.
George Mackay Brown: 'The Poet'
from *Selected Poems* by George Mackay Brown,
The Hogarth Press, 1977.
Reprinted by permission of the author and Chatto & Windus.
Sorley MacLean: 'Mac An T-Saoir Is Ros'
from *Spring-Tide and Neap-Tide: Selected Poems 1932-72*,
Canongate Publishing Ltd, 1977.
Reprinted by permission of the publisher.
Adrian Mitchell, 'Song In Space'
from *Nothingmas Day*, Allison & Busby, 1984.
Reprinted by permission.
Elma Mitchell: 'Good Old Days'
from *The Human Cage*, Harry Chambers/Peterloo Poets, 1979.
Reprinted by permission of the author.
John Montague: 'The Well Dreams'
from *The Dead Kingdom*, The Dolmen, Blackstaff, and Oxford University Presses, 1984.
Reprinted by permission of the author.
Edwin Morgan: 'The Poet'
from *Poems of Thirty Years*, Carcanet Press, 1982.
Reprinted by permission of the author.
Richard Murphy: 'Moonshine'
from *The Price of Stone* by Richard Murphy, 1985.
Reprinted by permission of the author and Faber and Faber Ltd.
Norman Nicholson: 'The Safe Side' from *Sea to the West*, Faber and Faber, 1981.
Reprinted by permission of the author.
Peter Porter: from 'Returning'
copyright © Peter Porter 1983; from Peter Porter's *Collected Poems*, 1983.
Reprinted by permission of Oxford University Press.
Paul Potts: 'Note'
from *Instead of a Sonnet*, Tuba Press, 1978.
Reprinted by permission of the author.
Kathleen Raine: 'Afternoon Sunlight Plays'
from *The Oval Portrait*, Hamish Hamilton, 1977.
Reprinted by permission of the author.

Peter Redgrove and **Penelope Shuttle:** 'A Man and His Wife'
from *The Hermaphrodite Album,* Fuller D'Arch Smith, 1973.
Reprinted by permission of the authors.
Edgell Rickword: 'Complaint After Psycho-Analysis'
from *Behind the Eyes: Selected Poems and Translations,* Carcanet Press, 1976. Reprinted by permission.
Anne Ridler: from 'Still Life'
from *The Golden Bird,* Faber and Faber, 1951.
Reprinted by permission of the author.
Vernon Scannell: 'The Men Who Wear My Clothes'
from *A Sense of Danger,* Putnam, 1962.
Reprinted by permission of the author.
Jon Silkin: 'The chisel grows heavy'
from *The Psalms with Their Spoils,* London, Routledge and Kegan Paul, 1980.
Reprinted by permission of the publishers.
C.H.Sisson: from 'The Regrets'
from *Collected Poems,* Carcanet Press, 1984.
Reprinted by permission of the publishers.
Sacheverell Sitwell: 'The Turn of the World'
from *An Indian Summer,* Macmillan, 1982.
Reprinted by permission of Macmillan, London and Basingstoke.
Elizabeth Smart: 'A Warning'
from *Eleven Poems,* Owen Kirton Publishing, 1982.
Reprinted by permission of the author's estate.
Iain Crichton Smith: 'Reflection'
from *River, River: Poems for Children,* Macdonald Publishers, 1978.
Reprinted by permission of the author.
Stephen Spender: 'Lost'
copyright © Stephen Spender 1946,
from *Collected Poems* by Stephen Spender,
Faber and Faber, 1955.
Reprinted by permission of Faber and Faber Ltd and Random House Inc.
R.S.Thomas: 'Self-Portrait'
from *Laboratories of the Spirit,* Macmillan, 1975.
Reprinted by permission of Macmillan, London and Basingstoke.
Anthony Thwaite: 'By the Sluice'
from *A Portion for Foxes,* Oxford University Press, 1977.
Reprinted by permission of the author.
Charles Tomlinson: 'Against Portraits'
copyright © Charles Tomlinson 1985;
from Charles Tomlinson's *Collected Poems,* 1985.
Reprinted by permission of Oxford University Press.
John Wain: 'My Name'
from *Poems 1949-1979* by John Wain, Macmillan, 1980.
Reprinted by permission of Macmillan, London and Basingstoke.
David Wright: 'Encounter in a Glass'
copyright © David Wright 1986. Printed by permission of the author.

Every effort has been made to trace
the holders of copyright.
The publishers will be pleased to hear from any
not acknowledged here.

SPECIAL ACKNOWLEDGEMENTS

Christopher and Sebastian Barker acknowledge a special debt of gratitude to the late Elizabeth Smart. Without her guidance and encouragement this book might never have been completed. Acknowledgement is also made to Sir Clive Sinclair, for his invaluable assistance at a crucial stage; and to John Fairfax, Bruce Bernard, Jonathan Barker, Pamela Clunies-Ross, Liam Miller, Eddie Linden and Gavin Henderson.